Vic Juris
Inside/Outside
Original Play-Along Modern Jazz Guitar Solos

By Vic Juris

Cover photography by Jimmy Katz
Recorded at Mountain Rest Studio, New Paltz, NY.
Guitar tracks played by Vic Juris
Bass - Jay Anderson
Drums - Tim Horner
All guitar music transcribed by Chuck Stevens

I0812327

Online Audio www.melbay.com/20849BCDEB

Audio Contents

1	All the Strings U.R. [2:54]	11	Little Steps [1:38]	21	Someday My Frog [2:30]
2	All the Strings U.R. (Rhythm only) [2:54]	12	Little Steps (Rhythm only) [1:38]	22	Someday My Frog (Rhythm only) [2:30]
3	Blue Joltice [1:56]	13	Pink Elephant Street [2:14]	23	Soul Art [1:20]
4	Blue Joltice (Rhythm only) [1:56]	14	Pink Elephant Street (Rhythm only) [2:14]	24	Soul Art (Rhythm only) [1:20]
5	Corey's Blues [1:20]	15	Rhythm's the Thing [2:20]	25	Stellar [2:26]
6	Corey's Blues (Rhythm only) [1:20]	16	Rhythm's the Thing (Rhythm only) [2:20]	26	Stellar (Rhythm only) [2:26]
7	First Voyage [3:36]	17	So Sensitive [3:42]	27	Tall Blues [2:18]
8	First Voyage (Rhythm only) [3:36]	18	So Sensitive (Rhythm only) [3:42]	28	Tall Blues (Rhythm only) [2:18]
9	Karate and Soul [4:34]	19	So What Else [2:02]	29	You Don't Know [4:42]
10	Karate and Soul (Rhythm only) [4:34]	20	So What Else (Rhythm only) [2:02]	30	You Don't Know (Rhythm only) [4:42]

Visit us on the Web at www.melbay.com — E-mail us at email@melbay.com

Contents

Introduction

It is with great pleasure Mel Bay Publications, Inc. releases this folio of solos, *Inside/Outside*, by Vic Juris. Vic is a true master of guitar and one of the brilliant minds in jazz. His concept of time and his harmonic sense put him in a league of his own. Vic played the solos in this collection with the student in mind. Each piece is based on the changes of popular jazz standards and will serve as great etudes for learning advanced jazz soloing techniques.

Students will be able to see how to build a solo, use tension and release ("outside" and "inside" playing), build an advanced jazz vocabulary, and develop a motive through a set of changes through careful study of these solos. It would be wise for students to not only learn the entire solo but also extract lines they especially like, master them in twelve keys, and apply them to their own solos.

Each etude has two play-along tracks found on the companion audio. One track is with Vic playing the solos found in the book and the other track is with rhythm section only. Students should first learn the solos and play with Vic to get the phrasing and articulation together (the ear will teach much more in this respect than the paper). Next, students should use the rhythm section track to venture out on their own. The rhythm section track can also be used for students to practice playing their own solos inspired by Vic's etudes.

Have fun learning these inspiring solos. This book, if used wisely, is sure to take any guitarist's playing to another level.

All the Strings U.R.

Track 1
Track 2 (rhythm only)

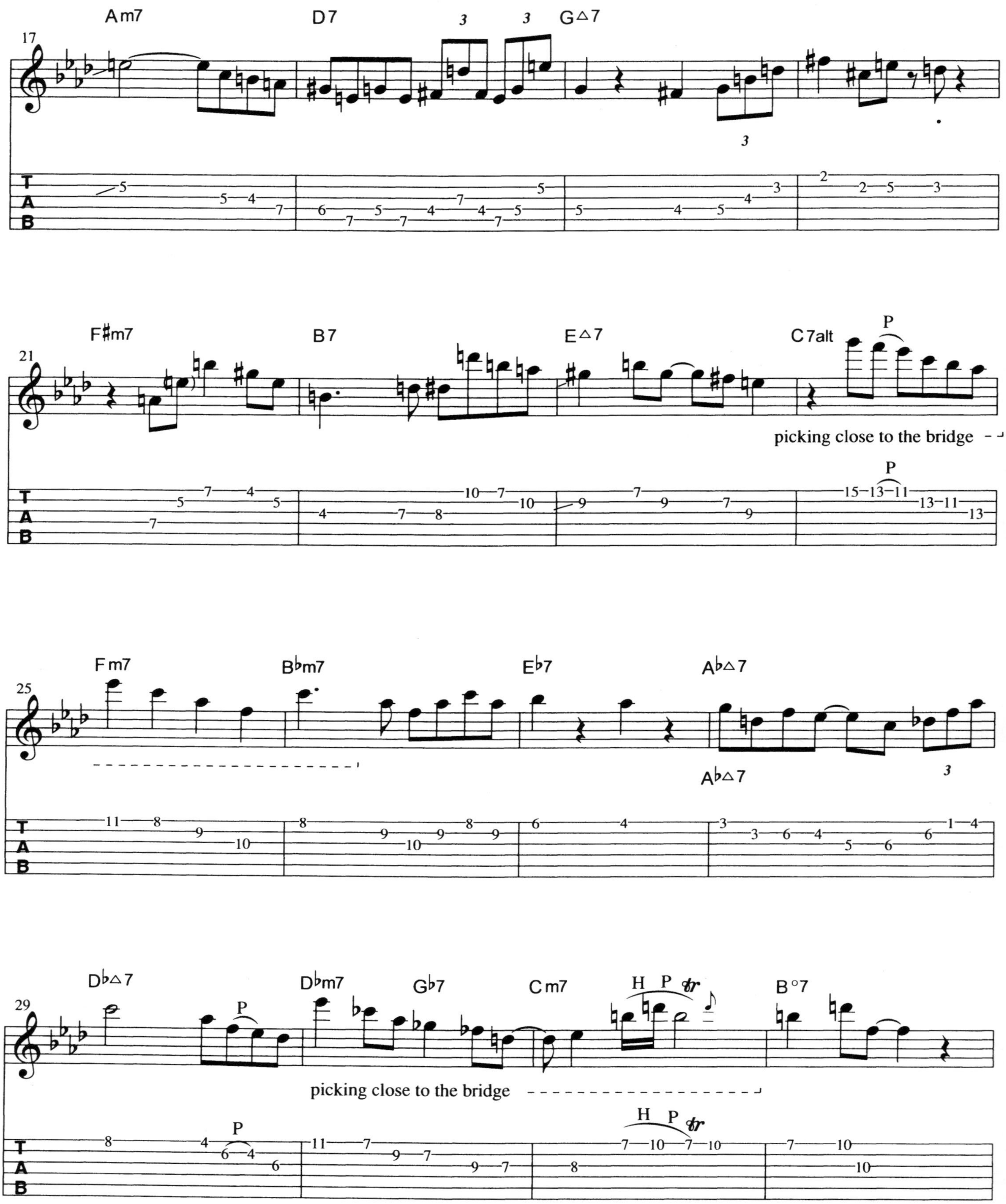
Am7
D7
G△7
F♯m7
B7
E△7
C7alt
picking close to the bridge
Fm7
B♭m7
E♭7
A♭△7
D♭△7
D♭m7
G♭7
Cm7
B°7
picking close to the bridge

B♭m7
E♭7
A♭△7
C7(♭9)
F m7
B♭m7
E♭7
A♭△7
D♭△7
D m7
G7
C△7
C m7
F m7
B♭7
E♭△7

49
A♭△7
Am7
D7
G△7
picking close to the bridge
53
Am7
D7
G△7
57
F♯m7
B7
E△7
C9(♯5)
picking close to the bridge
61
Fm7
B♭m7
E♭7
(Em7 laid back A7)
A♭△7
picking close to the bridge

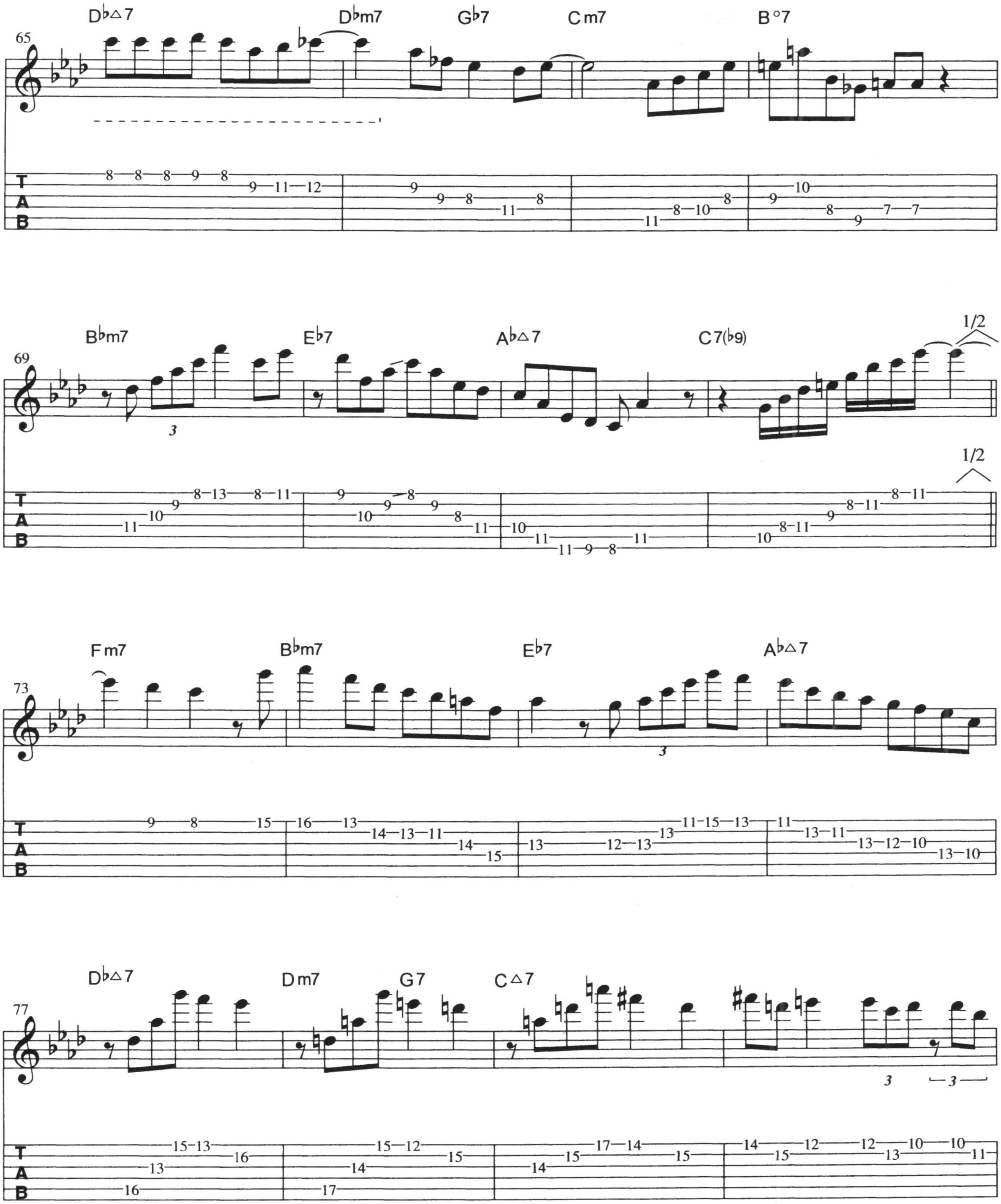
D♭△7 D♭m7 G♭7 Cm7 B°7
B♭m7 E♭7 A♭△7 C7(♭9)
1/2
Fm7 B♭m7 E♭7 A♭△7
D♭△7 Dm7 G7 C△7

81
Cm7
Fm7
B♭7
E♭△7
picking close to the bridge
85
A♭△7
Am7
D7
G△7
laid back
picking close to the bridge
89
Am7
P
D7
P
G△7
93
F♯m7
B7
E△7
C9(♯5)
even eigths
H
H
H
picking close to the bridge

Fm7
B♭m7
E♭7
A♭△7
D♭△7
D♭m7
G♭7
Cm7
B°7
B♭m7
E♭7
A♭△7
picking close to the bridge

Blue Joltice

Track 3
Track 4 (rhythm only)

18
Fm7
D∅
22
G7
Cm6
E♭m7
26
A♭7
D♭△7
D∅
30
G7
Cm7
D∅
G7
Cm7
sl.
1/2
T
A
B

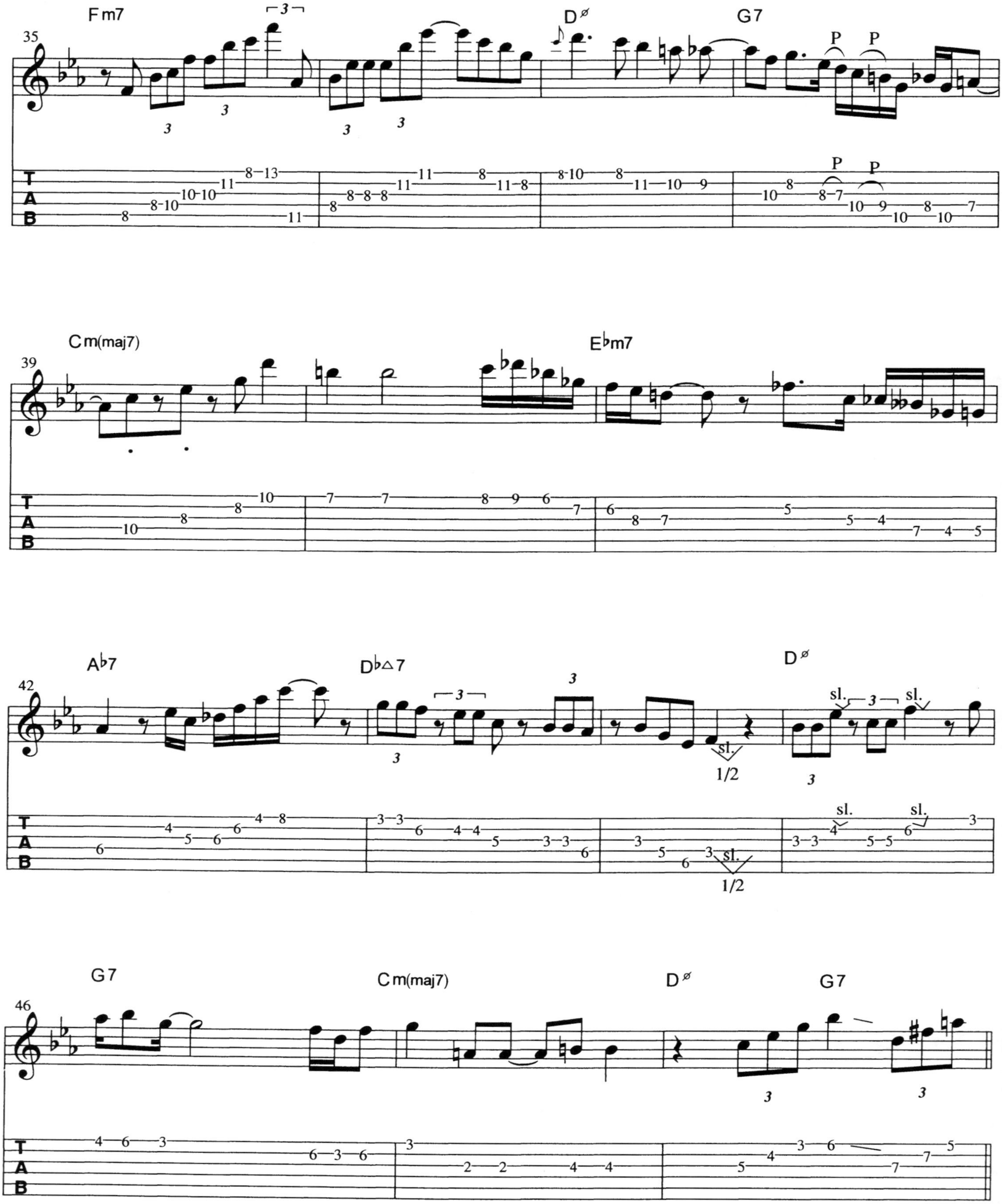
Fm7
D⌀
G7
P P
Cm(maj7)
E♭m7
A♭7
D♭△7
D⌀
sl.
1/2
G7
Cm(maj7)
D⌀
G7

Cm7
Fm7
sl. sl.
D⌀
G7
Cm(maj7)
sl.
1/2
E♭m7
A♭7
D♭△7
sweep
P

Corey's Blues

Track 5
Track 6 (rhythm only)

17
E♭7
E°7
B♭7
A7
A♭7
G7
21
Cm7
D♭7
G♭△7
A7
laid back
D△7
G7
C7
F7
25
B♭7
E♭7
B♭7
Fm7
B♭7
29
E♭7
E°7
B♭7
A7
A♭7
G7

33
Cm7 D♭7 G♭△7 A7 D△7 G7 C7 F7
picking close to bridge
37
B♭7 E♭7 B♭7 Fm7 B♭7
41
E♭7 E°7 B♭7 A7 A♭7 G7
laid back
45
Cm7 D♭7 G♭△7 A7 D△7 G7 Cm7 F7 B♭7

Track 7
Track 8 (rhythm only)

First Voyage

E♭7sus4
picking close to bridge
D♭7sus4
D7sus4
F7sus4

D7sus4
picking close to bridge
laid back
F7sus4
picking gradually
D7sus4
closer to the bridge
F7sus4

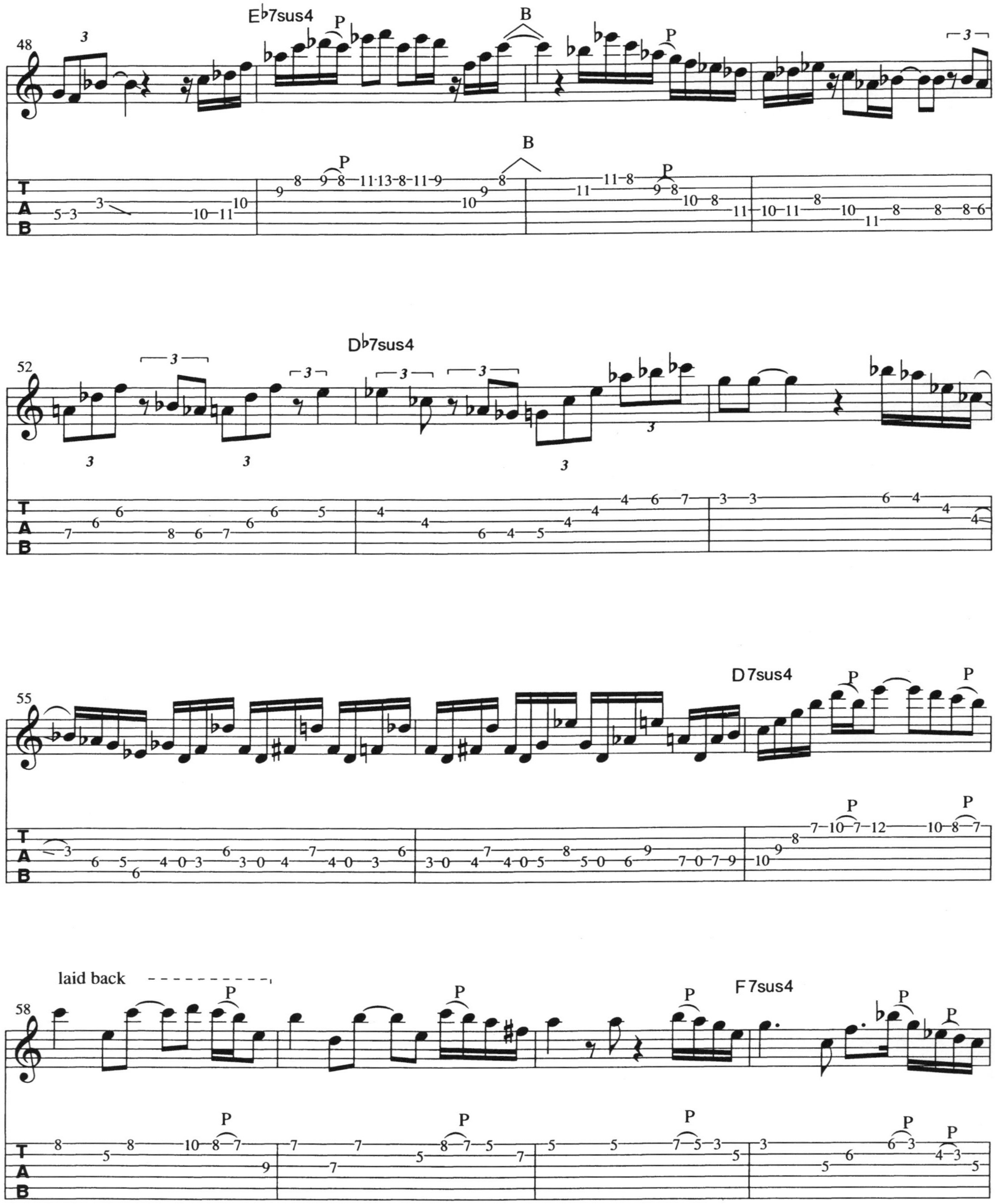
48
E♭7sus4
52
D♭7sus4
55
D7sus4
laid back
58
F7sus4

62
laid back
picking close to bridge
D7sus4
65
laid back
F7sus4
69
D7sus4
73

F7sus4
laid back
E♭7sus4
picking close to
the bridge
D♭7sus4
D7sus4

92
F7sus4
95
D7sus4

Track 9
Track 10 (rhythm only)

KARATE & SOUL

Fm7 E°7 E♭m7 /D♭ C⌀ F7
B♭m7 E♭7 E♭m7 A♭7 D♭△7 A7sus4
D△7 Em7 F♯m7 Gm7 C7 F♯m7 Bm7 Em7 A7
D△7 H Dm7 G7 Em7 E♭°7

Dm7 G7 C7 B7 B♭7 E13
E♭m7 B♭7+5 E♭m7 D7
D♭△7 G♭7 Fm7 E°7
E♭m7 /D♭ C⌀ F7 B♭m7 E♭7 E♭m7 A♭7

D♭△7
C7
B7
B♭7
H
E♭m7
B♭7+5
E♭m7
P
A♭7
D♭△7
G♭7
Fm7
E°7
E♭m7
/D♭
Cø
F7
B♭m7
E♭7
E♭m7
A♭7
D♭△7
C7
B7
B♭7

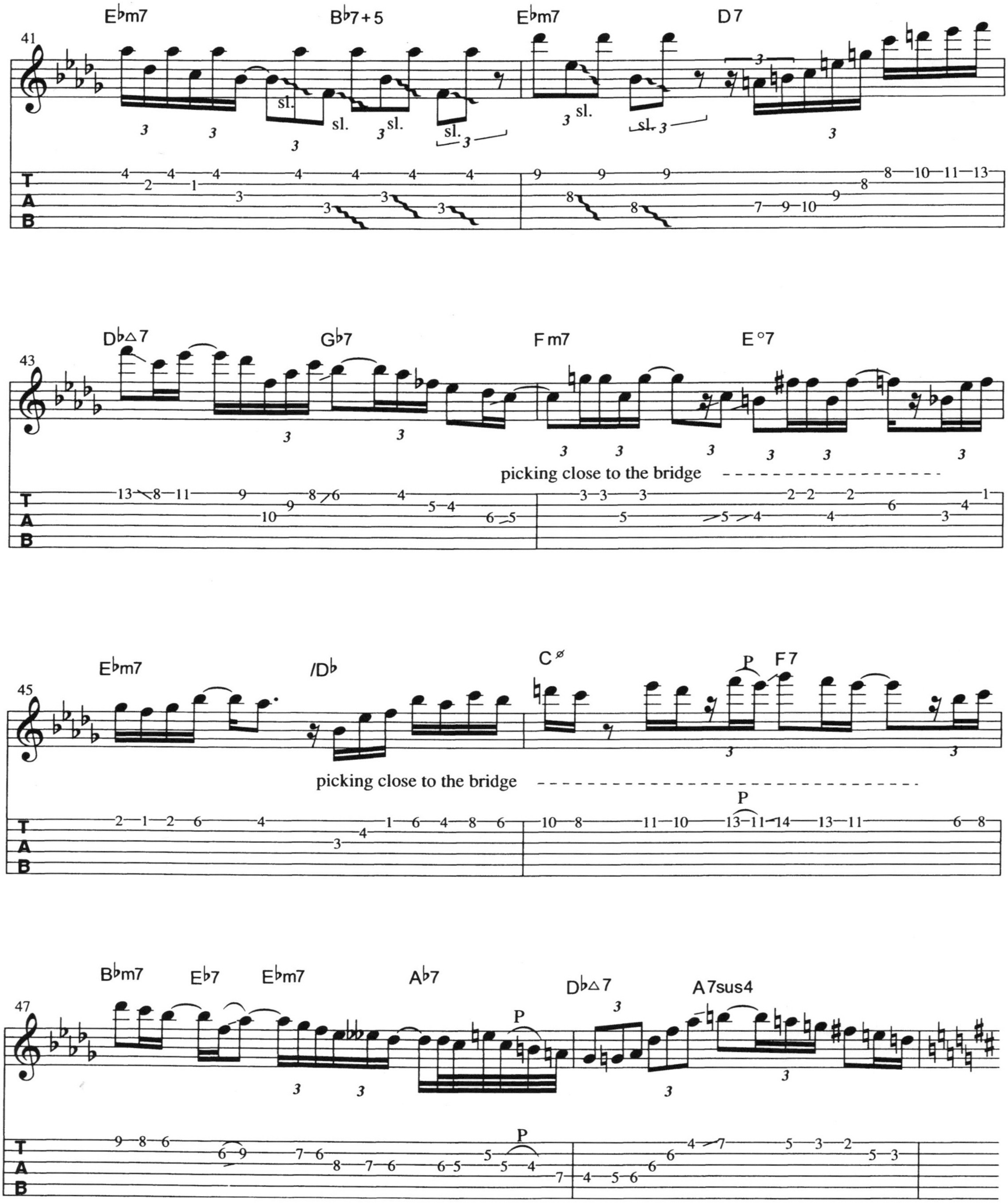
E♭m7
B♭7+5
E♭m7
D7
sl.
D♭△7
G♭7
Fm7
E°7
picking close to the bridge
E♭m7
/D♭
C⌀
F7
P
picking close to the bridge
B♭m7
E♭7
E♭m7
A♭7
D♭△7
A7sus4
P

D△7
Em7
F♯m7
Gm7
C7
F♯m7
Bm7
Em7
A7
D△7
Dm7
G7
Em7
E♭°7
Dm7
G7
C7
B7
B♭7
E13
E♭m7
B♭7+5

58
E♭m7
D7
D♭△7
G♭7
60
Fm7
E°7
E♭m7
/D♭
62
C⌀
F7
B♭m7
E♭7
E♭m7
A♭7
D♭△7(♯11)
rit.
T
A
B

This page has been left blank to avoid awkward page turns.

Track 11
Track 12 (rhythm only)

Little Steps

G△7 B♭7 E♭△7 Am7 D7 G△7 B♭7
E♭△7 F♯7 B△7 Fm7 B♭7 E♭△7 Am7 D7
G△7 C♯m7 F♯7 B△7 Fm7 B♭7 E♭△7
C♯m7 F♯7 B△7 D7 G△7 B♭7 E♭△7 Am7 D7

G△7 B♭7 E♭△7 F♯7 B△7 Fm7 B♭7
picking close to bridge
E♭△7 Am7 D7 G△7 C♯m7 F♯7
B△7 Fm7 B♭7 E♭△7 C♯m7 F♯7
B△7 D7 G△7 B♭7 E♭△7 Am7 D7
TAB

G△7 B♭7 E♭△7 F♯7 B△7 Fm7 B♭7
53
E♭△7 Am7 D7 G△7 C♯m7 F♯7
57
picking close to bridge
B△7 Fm7 B♭7 E♭△7
61

Track 13
Track 14 (rhythm only)

Pink Elephant Street

C△7
E♭△7
D7/C
D♭7/C
C△7
P
B7+5
B♭7
A7
Dm7
/C
B⌀
E7
Am7
/G
F♯⌀
B7
Em7
A7
Dm7
G7
D♭△7(♯11)
picking close to the bridge

C△7
laid back - - -
E♭△7/C
D7/C
D♭7/C
C△7
F7
Em7
A7
picking close to the bridge
Dm7
G7
C△7
Gm7
C7
Fm7
B♭7
E♭△7
Dm7
G7
picking

C△7
E♭△7/C
close to the bridge
D7/C
D♭7/C
C△7
F7
Em7
A7
Dm7
/C
B⌀
E7
Am7
/G
F♯⌀
B7
picking
Em7
A7
Dm7
G7
D♭△7(♯11)
close to the bridge
P

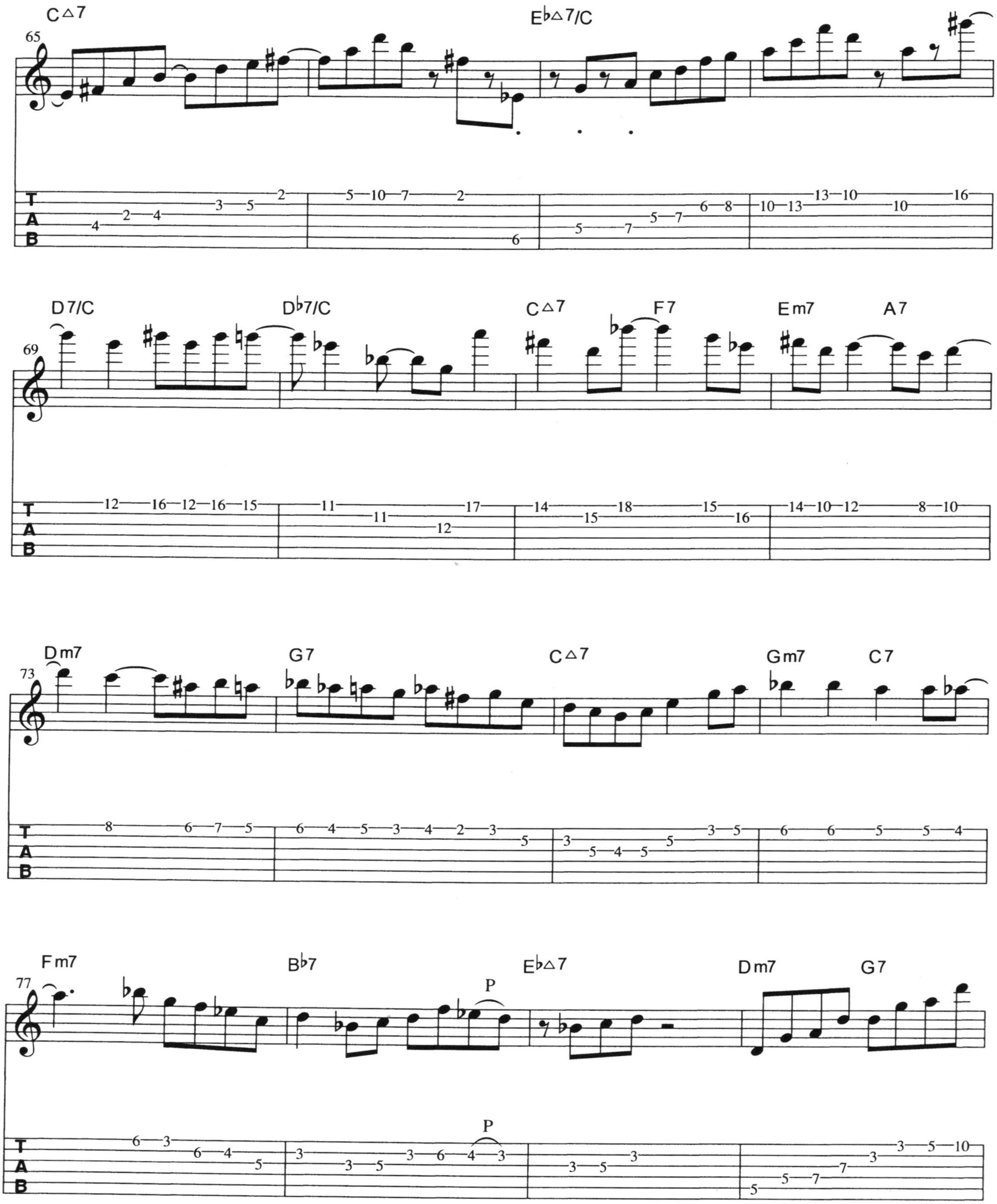
C△7
E♭△7/C
D7/C
D♭7/C
C△7
F7
Em7
A7
Dm7
G7
C△7
Gm7
C7
Fm7
B♭7
E♭△7
Dm7
G7

C△7
E♭△7/C
D7/C
D♭7/C
C△7
F7
Em7
A7
Dm7
/C
B∅
E7
Am7
/G
F♯∅
B7
Em7
A7
Dm7
G7
D♭△7(♯11)
rit.

Track 15
Track 16 (rhythm only)

Rhythm's the Thing

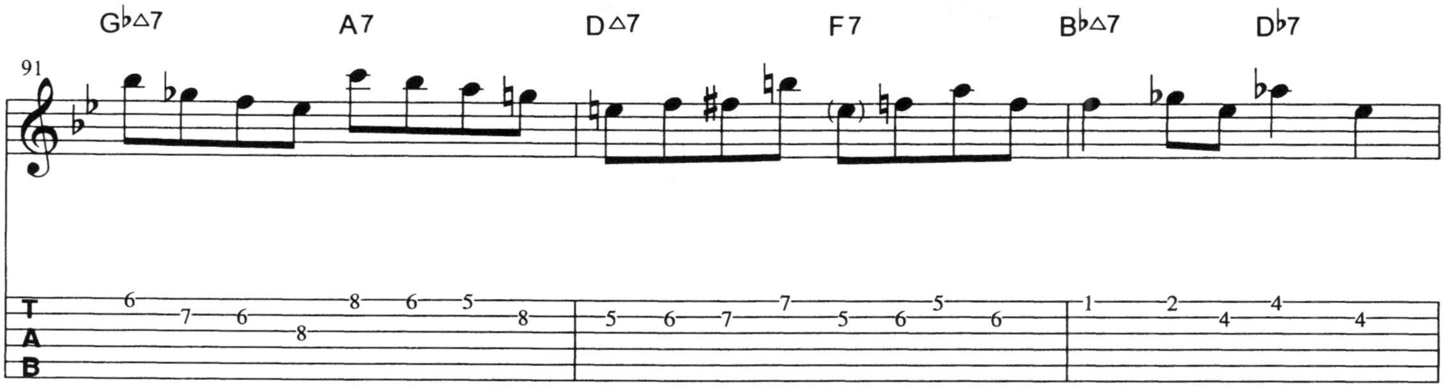
91
G♭△7
A7
D△7
F7
B♭△7
D♭7

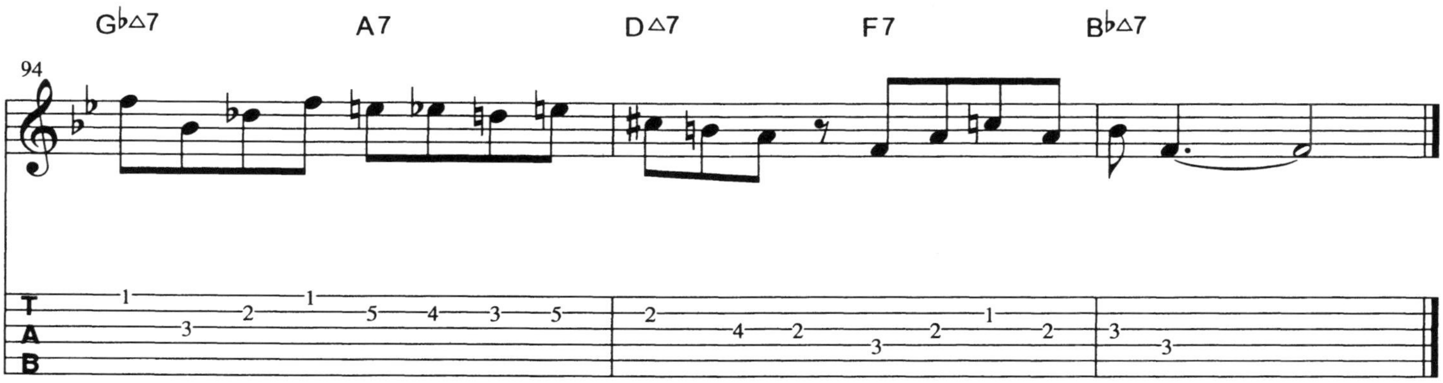
94
G♭△7
A7
D△7
F7
B♭△7

So Sensitive

Track 17
Track 18 (rhythm only)

D♭7
Cm7
B°7
B♭△7
E⌀
A7
Dm7
D♭7
picking close to the bridge
Cm7
picking close to the bridge
Bm7
E7

B♭△7
E∅
A7
Dm7
E∅
A7
Dm7
C♯°7
Cm7
G/B
B♭△7

E♭△7
H
Eø
A7
P
Dm7
D♭7
Cm7
B°7
B♭△7
Eø
A7
H
picking close to the bridge
Dm7
Dm7
D♭7
Cm7

58
Bm7
E7
B♭△7
62
E⌀
A7
Dm7
E⌀
A7
65
Dm7
C♯°7
picking close to the bridge
69
Cm7
G/B
HPH

*All Pull-offs
**All Hammer-ons

86
E∅ A7 Dm7 D♭7 Cm7
91
Bm7 E7 B♭△7 E∅ A7 Dm13

So What Else

Track 19
Track 20 (rhythm only)

21
Dm7
26
31
Dm7
H
36
P

41
P
46
P
E♭m7
51
56
Dm7

Dm7
P
P

E♭m7
P
Dm7
P

Someday My Frog Will Come

Track 21
Track 22 (rhythm only)

Cm7 F7 Fm7 B♭7 E♭△7 E⌀ A7
picking close to the bridge
Dm7 Gm7 Cm7 F7 B♭△7 D7+5
P
E♭△7 Dm7 D♭m7 Cm7 G7+5 Cm7
picking close to the bridge
F7 Dm7 Gm7 Cm7 F7
B
1/2

Dm7 Gm7 G♭△7 B△7♯11 B♭△7
D7+5 E♭△7 Dm7 D♭m7 Cm7 G7+5
Cm7 F7 Fm7 B♭7 E♭△7 E∅ A7
Dm7 Gm7 Cm7 F7 B♭△7 D7+5

67
E♭△7
Dm7
D♭m7
Cm7
G7+5
Cm7
72
F7
Dm7
Gm7
Cm7
F7
77
Dm7
Gm7
G♭△7
B△7♯11
B♭△7
D7+5
83
E♭△7
Dm7
D♭m7
Cm7
G7+5
T
A
B

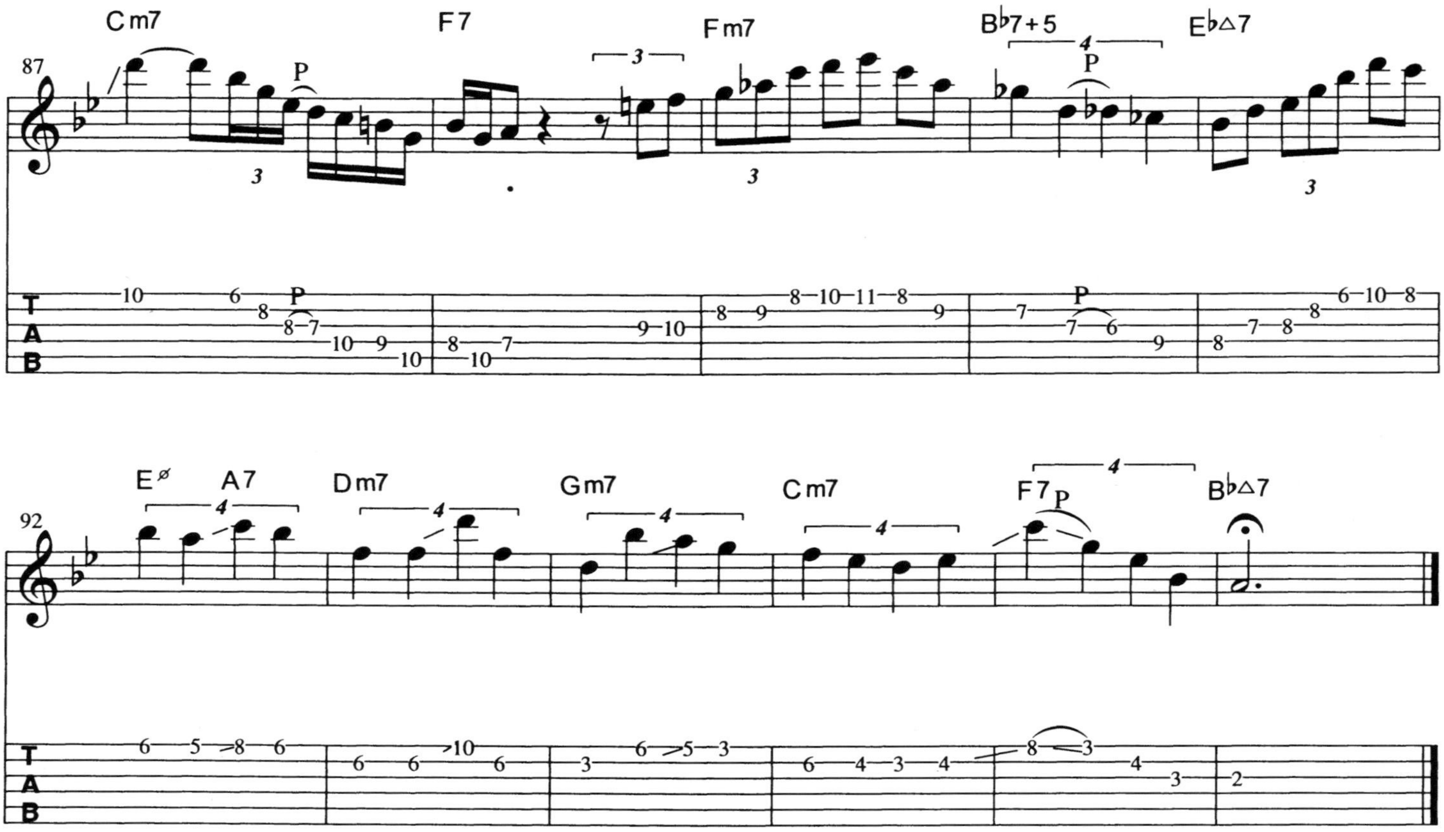
87
Cm7
F7
Fm7
B♭7+5
E♭△7
92
E∅
A7
Dm7
Gm7
Cm7
F7
B♭△7
TAB

Soul Art

Track 23
Track 24 (rhythm only)

E♭m7
A♭7
D♭△7
D⌀
G7
Cm7
Gm7
C7
F△7
Fm7
picking close to the bridge
B♭7
E♭△7
P
TAB

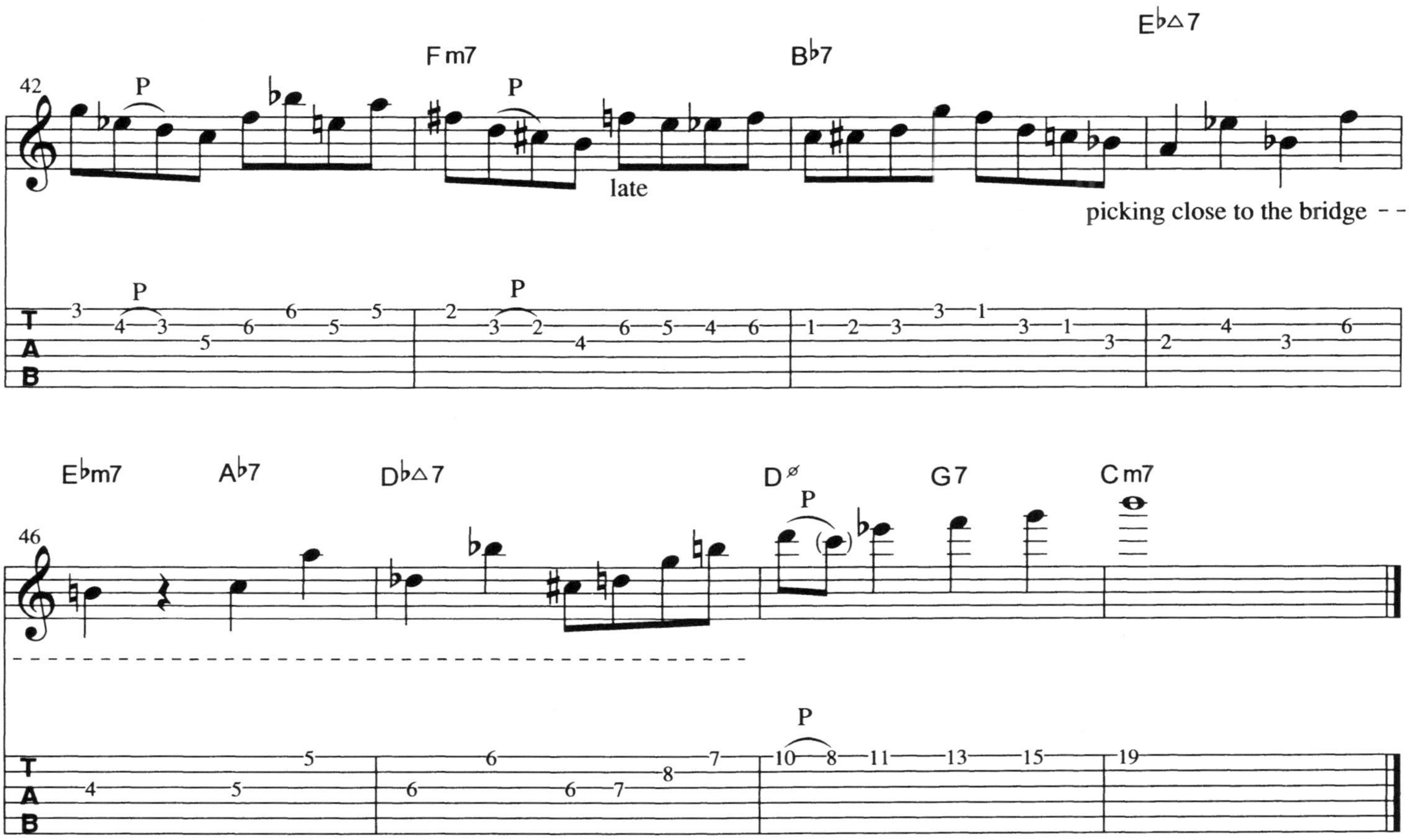

42
Fm7
B♭7
E♭△7
P
late
picking close to the bridge
46
E♭m7
A♭7
D♭△7
Dø
G7
Cm7

Track 25
Track 26 (rhythm only)

Stellar

A♭7(♯11)
A/B♭
B♭△7
E∅
A7
E♭m7
A♭7
D∅
G7
C♯m7
F♯7
Cm7
F7
B♭△7
A∅
Gm7
Fm7
E∅
A7
Cm7
F7
Fm7
B♭7
E♭△7
A♭7(♯11)

B♭△7
E⌀
A7
Dm7
B♭m7
E♭7
F△7
picking close to the bridge
E⌀
A7
A⌀
D7
G7+5
Cm7
A♭7(♯11)
A/B♭
picking close to the bridge
B♭△7
E⌀
A7
E♭m7
A♭7
Dm7
G7

C♯m7 F♯7 Cm7 F7 B♭△7 A⌀ Gm7 Fm7 E⌀
A7 Cm7 F7 Fm7 B♭7
late -
P
E♭△7 A♭7(♯11) B♭△7 E⌀ A7 Dm7
B
B♭m7 E♭7 F△7 E⌀ A7 A⌀ D7

G7+5
Cm7
A♭7(♯11)
A/B♭
B♭△7
Eø
A7
E♭m7
A♭7
Dm7
G7
C♯m7
F♯7
Cm7
F7
B♭△7

Tall Blues

Track 27
Track 28 (rhythm only)

G7
B
C7
B
B
G7
picking close to the bridge- - - -
D7

E♭7
D7
G7
vibrato
vibrato
G7
late
C7
vibrato
vibrato
G7

D7
E♭7
D7
G7
G7
C7

82
B
G7
86
P
D7
90
E♭7
D7
G7
T
A
B

YOU DON'T KNOW

Track 29
Track 30 (rhythm only)

G∅ C7 Fm7 B♭7 E♭m7 A♭7
D♭7 C7 Fm7 F7 B♭m7 E♭7
A♭△7 F7 B♭m7 E♭7 A♭△7
Dm7 G7 C△7 D♭7

laid back
G∅ C7 Fm7 D∅ G∅ C7
Fm7 G♭7 B7(♯11)
G∅ C7 Fm7 B♭7 E♭m7 A♭7 D♭7 G∅ C7
picking close to the bridge - -P
Fm7 G∅ C7 Fm7 D∅ G∅ C7

35
Fm7
G♭7
B7(♯11)
37
G⌀
C7
Fm7
B♭7
E♭m7
A♭7
39
D♭7
even
G⌀
C7
41
Fm7
D⌀
G⌀
C7
vibrato

Fm7 G♭7 B7(♯11)
G⌀ C7 Fm7 B♭7 E♭m7 A♭7
D♭7 G⌀ C7 Fm7 F7 B♭m7 E♭7
A♭△7 F7 B♭m7 E♭7

52
A♭△7
Dm7
G7
54
C△7
D♭7
G⌀
C7
even
57
Fm7
D⌀
G⌀
C7
59
Fm7
G♭7
B7(♯11)
P
B

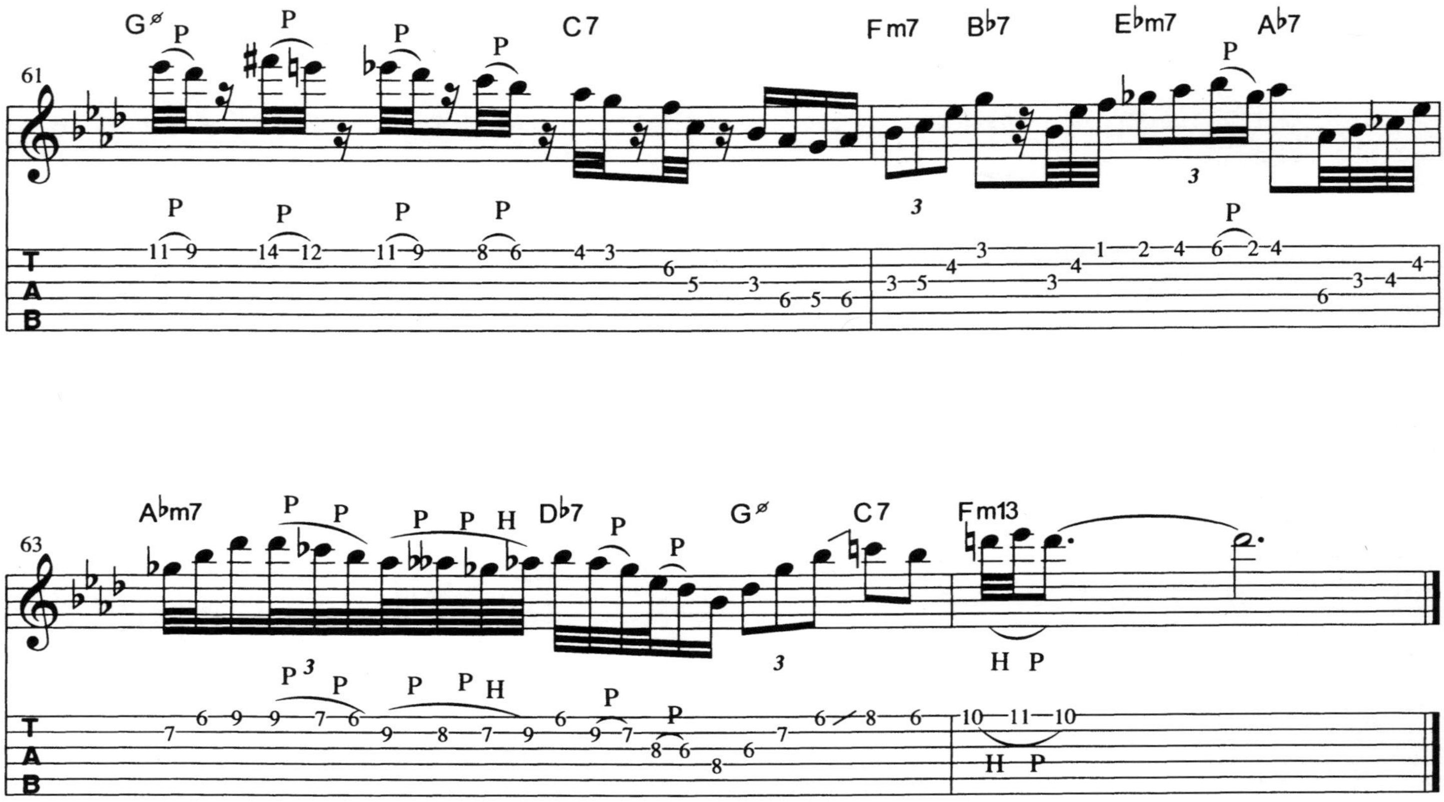
61
Gø
C7
Fm7
B♭7
E♭m7
A♭7
63
A♭m7
D♭7
Gø
C7
Fm13

Vic Juris

Born Victor E. Jurusz Jr., 26 September 1953, Jersey City, New Jersey, USA.

His guitar playing first began to attract attention in the early and mid-70s thanks to appearances and recordings with Phil Woods, Dizzy Gillespie, and Miroslav Vitous. Subsequently, he became part of the jazz fusion movement by joining keyboardist Barry Miles' group and also performing in duets with guitarist Larry Coryell. Vics ability to play in acoustic and electric jazz formats without loss of integrity ensured popular acceptance. Juris has also recorded and performed with: David Liebman, Freddie Hubbard, Gary Peacock, John Abercrombie, Bireli Lagrene and Lee Konitz to name a few.

Vic plays with fluent lyricism, choosing to seduce his listeners with subtle phrasing and engaging harmonies. Not surprisingly, therefore, his playing of ballads is particularly attractive, allowing the romantic element to blossom. In addition to his inventive playing Juris has also composed many songs, some of which he has recorded on the Steeplechase record label. He also has a new album on the Mel Bay Records label entitled *Second Look*.